Easter

The Resurrection of Jesus

We will see the cross at Easter.

We will go to the church at Easter.

Holy Trinity Church of England Moe
VICAR : THE REVEREND C.J CHAMBERS 1893
Evensong 7.00 pm
NOTICES
DEDICATED 3RD DECEMBER

We will see the eggs at Easter.

We will paint the eggs at Easter.

We will see the hats
at Easter.

We will see hot cross buns at Easter.

We will see fish

at Easter.

Easter is special for us.